By a Thread:
21 Tips on Resilience for the Partially Unraveled

NICOLETTE BLANCO

By a Thread

To contact the author, visit
www.nicoletteblanco.com.

Printed in the United States of America

ISBN: 0692725873
ISBN-13: 978-0692725870

DEDICATION

To my sisters, JoAnn and Ann Marie
Don't know what I'd do without you!

To my children, Conor and Erin
Love you both more than words.

CONTENTS

INTRODUCTION

It's been three days since writing and delivering the Words of Remembrance for my father's funeral service, and I sit here writing the introduction to a book on resilience. Isn't that the way life goes? It is an ongoing series of joyful and sorrowful events, and maybe the easiest thing to do is remind ourselves of the cycle, and remain confident that, no matter what the present circumstance, it can all change in a heartbeat—for better or worse, as they say. Perhaps this book should be just one page that states, "Trust the cycle." The joy will return; it always does if we allow it.

We know this intellectually, but our hearts sometimes have trouble believing it. We become stuck in the mud of present unfortunate circumstance, self-doubt, overwhelm, anxiety, and despair, and doubt the return of joy, love, celebration, freedom, and confidence. We allow other people's emotions to affect our own in ways that do not serve us or them. Paralyzed by inertia, we stagnate, and that becomes a stinky situation.

Funny how easy it is to believe that our joyful times are fleeting, yet fear that our sorrowful ones might be permanent, in the same way we shrug off our compliments but hold on for dear life to our criticisms.

When mired in negativity, we often choose things that give us immediate relief but make us feel worse in the long run, which can be the beginning of a nasty spiral. There are so many ways to soothe ourselves, and they don't have to include diving headfirst into a half gallon of chocolate ice cream. Not that I've ever done that.

Recently several people have asked me how it is I always manage to recover from setbacks. I had never really thought about it and, quite frankly, don't think my experiences are worse than most people's, but it is true that I don't get held down for long. Upon reflection, I realized there were many actions taken to get through the BOC (Bouts of Crap), and if people were asking, then perhaps they should be shared. Many times, the game changer wasn't an action at all, but a different way of looking at things, or a sudden "Aha!" moment. A change in perspective can do wonders.

My biggest realization is that it's not that complicated. We often turn the simple into the complex, which I truly believe is where people get stuck. Never underestimate the power of a healthy sense of humor. When it sounds like I am admonishing you about a particular behavior, know that I do so with a wink and a twinkle in my eye. You are strong, capable, and yes, resilient, even when you feel like you're drowning.

As you read this book, my hope is that one of these tips will resonate with you and be the starting point for positive change. It only takes one small step to begin the healing process. Pick one. Others can be added as you are ready. This isn't a race or competition. Your life is unfolding as it should, at its own pace, in its own jagged way.

Last week my father died, but today it is 70 degrees, with what e.e. cummings would call "a blue true dream of sky," and I'm going to revel in every minute of it. I wish you much revelry in all the bright spots of your life.

TIP #1: STOP SAYING "HOPE"

No, I don't mean you should be hopeless. Simply stop using the word "hope" in connection with things you want to accomplish or situations you want to change. "Hope" is best used in reference to things you have no control over, such as, "I hope it doesn't rain on my wedding day," or in reference to things that won't actually happen, such as, "I hope to wake up tomorrow morning, thirty years younger, knowing everything I know now, and finding James Spader making breakfast in my kitchen." Not happening.

Hope is the antithesis of action. In my own case, I had hoped to write a book for a long time, but not a word was written until I said, "I'm writing a book." Don't just hope to do something. Actually do it, and start now.

Same holds true for the word "try."
Don't try to remember that; just remember it.

What have you been hoping to do?

What has been holding you back?

What is your first step?

When will you do it?

Date: _____

TIP # 2: CLIMB A MOUNTAIN

Perhaps you're hoping that's a metaphor, but no. It's time to actually break out (or buy) the hiking boots, go outside, and climb a damn mountain. Relax, it doesn't need to be Mount Everest, but make it something a little harder than you've done before. Never hiked? Excellent. That means you have a world of choices, and they'll all be the hardest climb you've ever done. Live in a flatland? Simply walk or run a little faster, harder, or farther. Don't be a wimp about this. You are more capable than you think you are!

Don't confuse a challenge with a dare. This isn't about the adrenaline rush of skydiving or bungee jumping; it's about physical effort. The feeling will be so sweet when you succeed, and if you don't succeed the first time, keep at it. The eventual success will be even sweeter.

*Don't **hope** to do it someday. Make a plan and do it (see Tip #1).*

How will you challenge yourself?

What has been holding you back?

What is your first step?

When will you do it?

Date: _____

TIP#3: EMBRACE IMPERFECTION

Nothing kills action faster than perfectionism. How many of us have kept our innovative ideas, books, business concepts, artistic creations, and other possible gems hidden because we thought they weren't good enough? We read, observe, and experience great works and think, "I'll share my gifts when I get them just right," forgetting about the bold failures most masters experience along the way. At the very least, our favorite masterpieces were step-by-step processes; their creators started with an idea, experimented with different strategies, and finally saw the result of their hard work.

Now what if most of us don't have that masterpiece in us? Maybe all we have is the ability to reach one other person with our gifts. Isn't that enough? Maybe that person takes the seed of inspiration we've sown, changes her life, transforms her family, or creates the masterpiece that never would have existed without us.

How great is that?

How has perfectionism held you back?

What one project will you imperfectly begin (and finish!)?

What is your first step?

When will you begin?

Date: _____

TIP#4: KILL THE SNOOZE ALARM HABIT

Set the alarm for the time you actually need to get up, then GET UP. Repeatedly hitting the snooze button is like ripping off a bandage, putting a fresh one on the same spot, ripping it off five minutes later, and repeating the process three or four times. Every time hurts a little more and the pain lasts a little longer. Every time you hit the snooze button, your body resets its sleep cycle, which is why you typically feel more tired at the subsequent "snoozes." The resulting tired, groggy feeling can last from two to four hours after rising, making the day much less productive.

Settling into a regular sleep pattern, which includes weekends, is the best way to feel rested and refreshed in the morning. It allows the body to find a rhythm of hormone and temperature regulation that sets the stage for increased alertness and productivity throughout the day.

If you have children waking you up or other factors disrupting your sleep during the night, it is even more important not to snooze before rising. Allow the longest sleep stint possible or you're simply making a bad situation even worse.

Do yourself a favor and only rip the bandage off once.

Ok, this one's simple: what time do you REALLY need to get up?

Set your alarm for _____ AM/PM.

GET UP

TIP#5: DON'T SET YOUR EMOTIONAL THERMOSTAT TO YOUR CHILDREN'S TEMPERATURE

I once heard a woman say that she was only ever as happy as her least happy child, and I thought, WHAT? Yes, as parents we desire to protect and comfort our children, but we do them no favors by allowing ourselves to be woven into whatever emotional tangle they are wrestling with.

Our children do not need us to experience their emotions with them; they need us to be solid, constant, and loving. They need us to show them there is a light at the end of the tunnel, and that we will support them through it, even if at times that support looks more like walking away.

This one took me a while to figure out and still takes practice. Begin by picking one small struggle that your child is experiencing and try to let it go. Allow them to grow and figure it out on their own, with you there to support them if needed, but not to hover, fret, or offer unsolicited advice. Keep stretching until you work up to the big ticket item that's keeping you up at night. Not easy, and doubtful it will work every night, but remember: your light helps your children more than your worry ever will.

~ Sweet Dreams ~

What one concern can you let go of regarding your children?

Why has this been difficult to do?

How has your worrying impacted you or your children?

Slow breath in. Slow breath out. Repeat several times.

Let it go.

TIP#6: BE. HERE. NOW

How many times has rehashing old wounds brightened your day? I used to rehash old arguments thinking that somehow, this time, I'd win. Better yet, sometimes I would have arguments with people in my head over things that hadn't even happened yet. I have lost perfectly wonderful days by focusing my energy on another time and place, until I realized that nothing is more important than—nothing even exists other than—here and now. If we focus solely on being present, open, and content in each moment, then we end up with a fulfilled life. The past is over and the future does not exist. This is it.

Once that truly sunk in, I was weightless, free, even euphoric. I realized I have the power to choose how I want to feel in every moment, which means I have control over my entire life. So, be here. Really be here, now, and let your spirit soar for this moment,

and this one, and this one, and this one...

What old wound do you continue to rehash?

Why?

How has this impacted your life?

How would it feel to release it?

Let go.

TIP #7: PURSUE **YOUR** DREAMS

We are bombarded with daily messages about, among many things, what we should want, do, be, and look like. These pressures are so pervasive that it becomes all but impossible to discern what we *should* want from what we *do* want. Are you chasing someone else's dream? Maybe you're a teen heading off to college in pursuit of your parents' dream, but it doesn't make your heart sing; or you're in your twenties or thirties climbing the wrong ladder; or you're in your forties or fifties and on the top rung but still seeking fulfillment; or you're retired and wondering what happened.

Dreams and goals are wonderful things, but only when they're yours. How amazing to be young and loving your job, middle-aged and feeling confident and inspired, or older and feeling a deep sense of satisfaction and accomplishment.

It's easy to know if you're on the right track. Just check in with your gut. It knows.

Always.

What would you like to pursue, personally or professionally, but haven't?

Why?

What would it take to begin?

When will you take the first step?

Date: _____

TIP #8: GRIEVE

On what would have been our twentieth wedding anniversary, I was feeling acutely raw and wounded. While subsequent anniversary dates have not been particularly emotional, the divorce had been finalized just a year prior, and the feelings of sadness and loss, as well as the longing for what could have been, had bubbled to the surface. I was missing the celebration that two decades earlier I had assumed would take place on this day. The emotions were not to be denied.

And so I made a conscious decision to simply let myself feel it that day. There would be no attempt to lift my spirits, no mountain climbed, no inspirational book read. I nestled in the crap and made a home there for the day.

Our emotions do not exist for us to repress them. They are reminders that we are alive and that the people, places, and events in our lives matter. That's a good thing. The suggestions in the book are not meant to imply that our difficult emotions should be repressed; they are my humble suggestions of simple things that may help break the cycle when it all feels like too much. It's essential to feel the full range of emotions when they arise, but they don't need to take up permanent residence in your home. Grief can be scary, but it will haunt you forever if you don't move through it.

Go there. Feel it. Move on. Repeat as necessary.

What have you been afraid to grieve?

What emotions would this bring up?

Who can support you through this process?

How would making peace with this event or situation change your life?

TIP #9: BE YOUR CLOSEST FRIEND

Think of the people closest to you in your life. If they were all coming over for dinner, what would your home look like? What would be served? How would you speak to them? Would you judge them? I'm guessing that your home would be clean and a tasty meal would be served. They would be spoken to respectfully and you would be a source of encouragement for them through any perceived failures.

Do you treat yourself this way? Do you allow yourself to live in a warm and welcoming space? What do you feed yourself? How do you speak to yourself when you make a mistake? Do you judge yourself for your failures or congratulate yourself for daring to try?

Never lose sight of the gift you are. You are your closest friend and worst enemy, and the one you nurture will be the loudest voice in your head and heart.

It's time to break out the good china.

How do you treat yourself as "less than" and why?

How does this impact your life?

In what way will you treat yourself better?

Begin now.

TIP #10: BREATHE

The crazier life feels, the more important this is. We all have specific things that happen to us when we don't take time to breathe and relax. For me, it's losing the car keys. For a while there it was nearly a daily occurrence. How ridiculous was it to spend an hour every day searching for something that's critical in my life?

Our entire system slows down by simply spending 5-10 minutes on slow, deep, relaxed breathing, focusing on the breath, and allowing other thoughts to come and go. This small act provides amazing benefits, from increased clarity of thought to a reduction in stress hormones. It is a wonderful practice right before meals, because stress shuts down our digestive process and sets the stage for a host of digestive issues.

So, when life gives you lemons…

Just breathe.

What are the most stressful parts of your day?

How would they improve if you approached them in a more relaxed and focused manner?

Set reminders for this practice until it becomes a habit.

Breathe.

TIP #11: SOW SOMETHING

Plant a garden, an idea, a kernel of your truth, or that seed of inspiration from Tip #3, but sow *something*. All it takes is one step. That's it. Take the step, breathe, release the worry. The only certainty is that there will be no outcome if you do not take the first step. Release what you expect should happen and allow what unfolds. That's the beauty (and the fun!): watching what unfolds. Be open to the resources showing up in your life.

Life is more about allowing than doing. Sure, it takes action to set things in motion, but yours are not the only hands on the wheel. Remember, you only need to do three things: take the step, breathe, and allow.

GO!

What have you been afraid to begin?

Why?

How has this impacted your life?

How would it feel to take that first step?

When will you take the step?

Date _____

TIP #12: REAP SOMETHING

How often do you plant the seeds and tend the garden, but
don't reap the harvest? Why? Perhaps you don't think you
deserve it, or are afraid of the responsibilities that come with
success, or think the results aren't good enough, or *you* aren't
good enough. Maybe you're afraid that people will truly see
you, and won't like what they see. But if what people are
seeing isn't the real you—I mean the open, authentic,
miraculous, one-of-a-kind *you*—then what's the point?

True connection and fulfillment cannot happen when your
heart is lying under a rock. Living in authenticity will liberate
you beyond your wildest dreams. Take chances, succeed, fail:
reap something and see what happens. Whatever you do,
don't let the crop wither and die.

Oh look, it's harvest time!

What unfinished business do you have in your life?

Why is this incomplete?

How is this impacting your life?

How would it feel to complete it?

When will you begin?

Date _____

TIP #13: FORGIVE

An ongoing process. Where to start: friends, family, strangers, circumstances, yourself. It took me a long time to realize that forgiveness has nothing to do with the other person. And frankly, I still remind myself of this quite often. *It's not about them.* It's all about you, and your ability to be free.

Have you noticed how often the people you haven't forgiven have moved on, while you are completely stuck in resentment? Kinda crazy, don't you think? Forgiveness is a gift. Not to them, to you.

Unwrap it.

Who do you need to forgive?

How is this resentment affecting your life?

How would it feel to forgive and let go?

If needed, who can support you though this process?

TIP #14: ASK "WHAT I CAN LEARN FROM THIS EXPERIENCE?"

Be careful with this one. I once asked myself this in the midst of a particularly rough patch and my sole response was, "Nothing, you asshole." Sometimes a little distance is required.

Every moment of despair or inspiration, love or hate, good or bad—every moment of life—teaches us something. Even though I couldn't always see it in the moment, knowing this is true often got me through. I knew some day the distance would be great enough and the golden nugget of wisdom would shine.

What is life teaching you right now? The answer is in your heart, not your head. You will feel the shift when it happens, so don't overthink it. Be patient and trusting. If no answer is coming, that just means you're not ready. The answer will come in due time. Be patient; be trusting.

Wait for it.

Write down every positive thing you can learn from your present experience:

TIP #15: GET HAPPY FIRST

So often people think, "When I get that new job, more money, a bigger house, a new car… then I'll be happy." Unfortunately, it doesn't work that way. Happiness does not come from external success; it comes from within. I'm not talking about a yeehaw, woohoo, jumping-up-and-down kind of happiness (although that's fun too!). I'm talking about a deep contentment and connection with yourself, regardless of external circumstances.

It's easy to be happy when everything around you is wonderful, but rarely is everything around you wonderful when you are in the midst of internal turmoil. While you're waiting for life to turn around, your inner turmoil is shouting, "I'm not ready yet." It's ok to feel broken, but allow the light to come into those broken spaces.

In the Japanese art of Kintsugi, broken bowls are mended by filling the cracks with gold and other precious metals. It is believed that the bowls' brokenness is what makes them beautiful. What are you filling your broken places with: love, light, and inspiration, or anger, resentment, and blame? Let the light in whenever you can, and slowly (or quickly) the world around you will change and the fog will lift. The inner work must precede the outer.

Start with the heart.

What have you felt you need to have, do, or be in order to be happy?

How has this belief impacted your life?

Try to imagine yourself happy without these things. Take your time with this.

Write about all the ways your life would change if you had a deep sense of peace and contentment.

Begin by letting one small ray of light into one of those broken places.

TIP #16: HONOR THE MORNING

Remember when we couldn't begin working until we GOT TO WORK? No glow of email under the covers, continual text messages, or non-urgent phone calls. No scrolling through social media sites. No intrusions from the outside world.

I often hear people say that they don't have time to slow down and set their intentions for the day. However, many of them manage to read and respond to email and text messages, as well as check favorite social media sites, before ever hitting the shower. Our morning rituals set the tone for the day, so it's no wonder many people live the entire day the same way they began it: distracted and stressed. How can the day go well when it begins with stressful work emails or news of world atrocities? How can you be present with yourself and those around you with constant distraction?

Being intentional doesn't need to be time consuming. Simple things: breathing deeply for 60 seconds, reading an inspirational quote, using time in the shower to think of all you're grateful for, giving your full attention to those around you, writing down your plan for the day, laughing in the midst of family chaos. Whatever centers and grounds you will work.

Be intentional about the morning. You may not be able to change the daily tasks that await you, but you can change the way you feel about them, and that changes everything.

Rise 'n' shine!

How would your day change if it began relaxed and focused?

What are the barriers to beginning your day with intention?

How can you overcome or work around at least one of these barriers?

What one intentional practice will you incorporate into your morning routine?

When will you begin?

Date _____

TIP #17: STOP THE RESISTANCE

Oh, the time I spent with one foot on the pedal and one foot on the brake, wanting to move forward but afraid to truly commit, knowing that change would bring discomfort. Heck, I was already uncomfortable and sometimes downright miserable, both personally and professionally. Who wants to add more angst to that?

Once I finally stopped the resistance and made a leap in one area of my life, subsequent action was that much easier. Sure, initially it is new territory, rife with instability and second guessing. But then the new world becomes familiar and free. You knew this would happen all along, but it's hard to remember when you're stuck in wet cement. Just pull your foot out before it dries.

It's ok if you lose a flip flop along the way.

What have you been resisting?

Why?

What do you think would happen if you stopped the resistance?

Slowly ease your foot off the brake.

TIP #18: CONNECT TO SOMETHING GREATER

I am more of a spiritual than religious person. Churchgoing has been spotty, and I left the Catholic Church, in which I was raised, many years ago. But through it all, a deep sense of connection has remained. Some days it was connection to a higher power, other days to friends, family, and the community around me, and still others to the beauty of nature. The "what" doesn't matter, but the connection does. Without it we are like sown seeds deprived of sunlight and water. Isolation can be paralyzing, while connection is liberating and inspiring.

Don't confuse isolation with solitude. Times of solitude can be our most connected times. It's not the people around us that creates connection; it's the feeling—the feeling of being grounded yet free, focused and inspired, confident and relaxed.

The opportunities to connect to things that are greater or lesser than ourselves are ever-present.

Plug in and turn on the light!

To what or whom *do* you feel connected?

To what or whom would you *like* to feel connected?

What steps can you take to begin creating connection where there presently is none?

When will you take the first step?

Date _____

TIP #19: CELEBRATE OTHERS' SUCCESS

How easy it is to be resentful of other people's success when we are struggling, to look at them with envy instead of joy, and believe that their success somehow steals the spotlight from others, or that their wealth takes from those who have less. That envy plunges us further into despair, cutting off all possibility of realizing our true potential. Plus, those beliefs are not true. Nothing could be further from the truth. There is plenty for everyone.

There is no set timeline to reach your dreams. Your life is like no other, and concern about how your personal progress compares to others will stifle any forward movement. Jealousy and envy are like anchors of death and will surely drown your desires. Only in joy and celebration does growth occur.

Let the party begin!

How do you truly feel when witnessing others' success?

If your responses were negative, how has this impacted your life?

What beliefs about yourself would you need to release in order to feel joy when witnessing others' success?

Beliefs are deep seated. Explore one negative belief and its roots.

As your beliefs about yourself and your celebrations of others change, watch your life change!

TIP #20: CULTIVATE AN ATTITUDE OF GRATITUDE

So your life is in the toilet, and I'm telling you to be grateful. Yes. Even in the darkest of times, there are things to be grateful for if you look hard enough. That's the key: look hard enough.

Some days perhaps all you find to be grateful for is a sunny sky, or the fact that your car started, but those are pretty good things! As luck would have it, the more you focus on the positive, the more good you will notice, and more will come your way. You just need to start the process.

How to start? Simple. Get a notebook or journal and keep it by your bed. Every night write down five things you are grateful for *from that day*. That's it. Night is the time we typically obsess over all the negatives, and this is a great way to get your mind focused on the positive before sleep, so you *can* sleep!

Although this is the one of the last tips, it may be the one that was the most helpful for me.

Get writing!

What five things are you grateful for today?

TIP #21: KNOW YOU ARE ENOUGH

'nuff said.

CONCLUSION

We all process information and experiences uniquely. While each of these 21 tips has helped me at some point in my life, you will discover many others that work for you in your unique circumstances. My hope is that you say "yes" to the solutions discovered along the way, and have the courage to take that first step into a new habit, perspective, or perhaps whole life. Only you know what's right. Resilience is a process, not a destination, and putting one foot in front of the other is often all it takes.

As a Health Coach, I have discovered that it is often the inability to overcome setbacks, or a lack of belief that the present situation can truly change, which halts progress. True health is not solely about eating right and exercising; it is in large part about how we feed ourselves mentally, emotionally, and spiritually, and the ability to be resilient in the face of adversity. This is step one in the healing process. It's all about continual growth, and it's never finished.

If you enjoyed reading this book and found the suggestions helpful, I would love to hear from you. You can contact me directly and learn more about my health coaching programs at www.nicoletteblanco.com. Until then, I wish you much love, light, and laughter on your journey.

Made in the USA
San Bernardino, CA
20 July 2016